LET'S HAVE A ~~MELTDOWN~~ LAUGH

Written by Debbie L. Hepner

Illustrated by Katie Risor

This is a work of fiction. Any resemblance to actual events or persons, living or dead, is entirely coincidental.

Let's Have a Meltdown/Laugh - by Debbie L. Hepner, Illustrated by Katie Risor

Paperback ISBN 978-1-7375067-8-2
Hardback ISBN 978-1-7375067-9-9
The illustrations in this book were made digitally.

This book is dedicated to all the sweet kids
out there who just need to LET IT OUT!

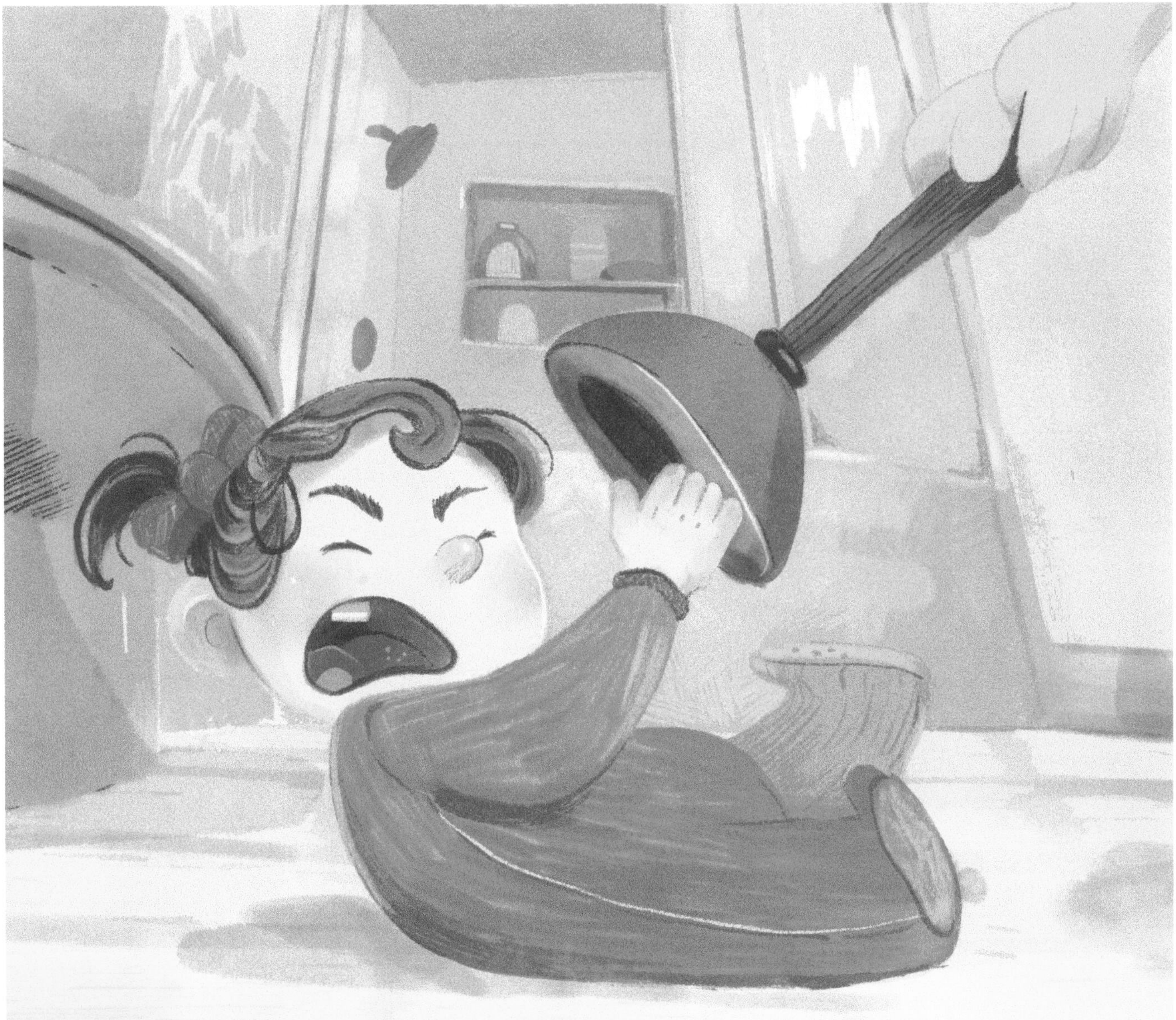

"No! You can't put the plunger on your face!"

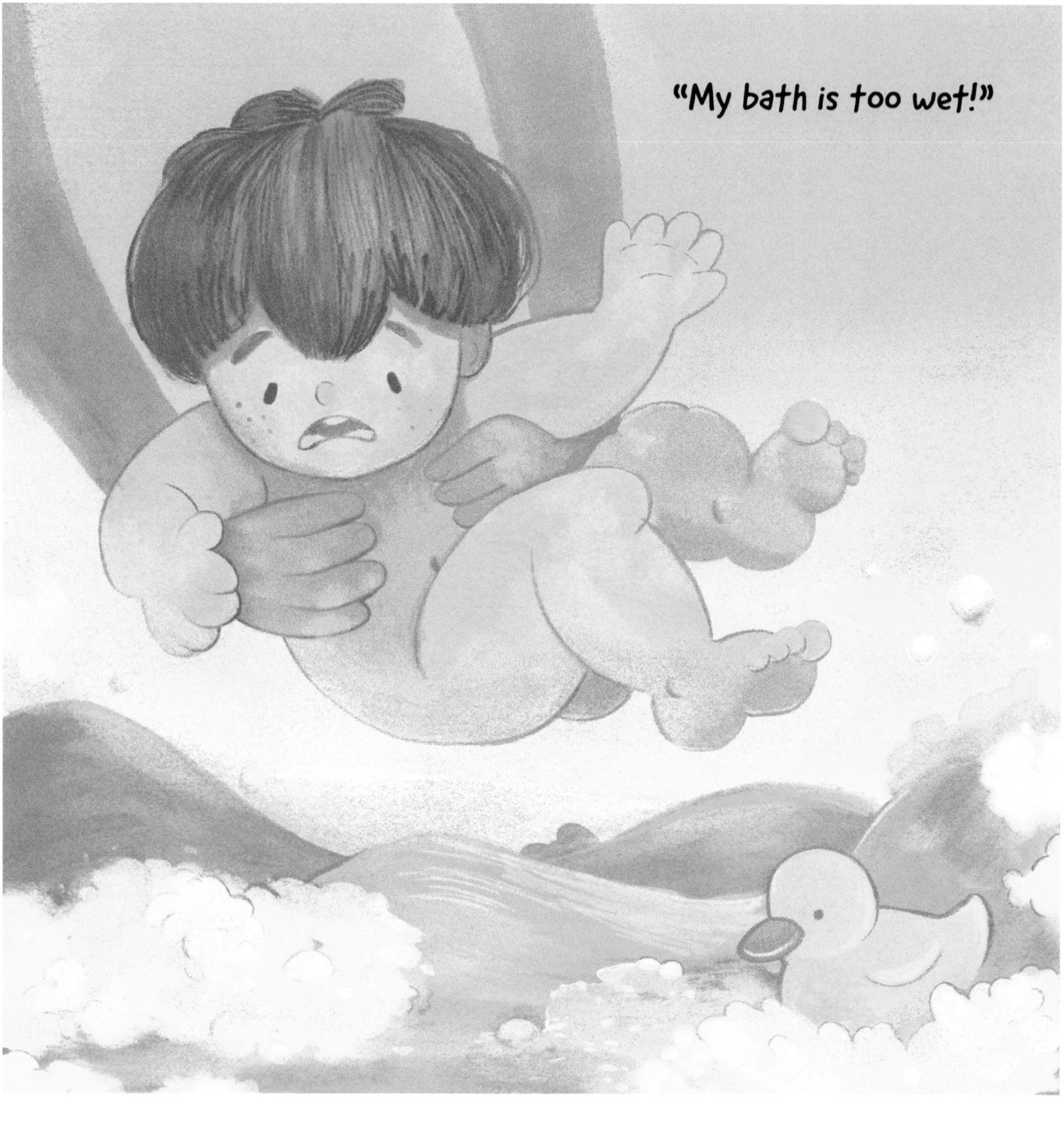

"My bath is too wet!"

"No sweetie the dog can't drive you to daycare."

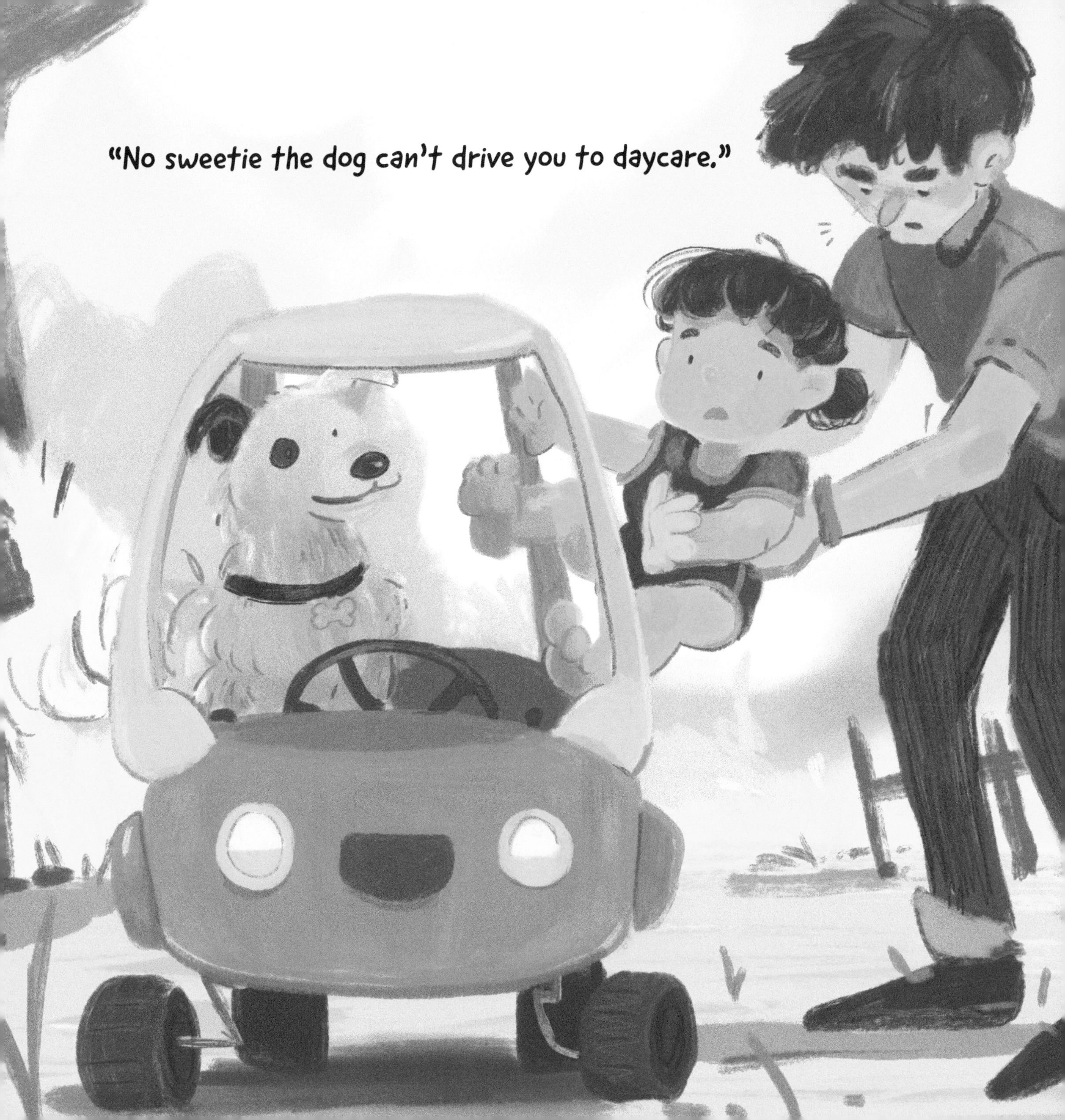

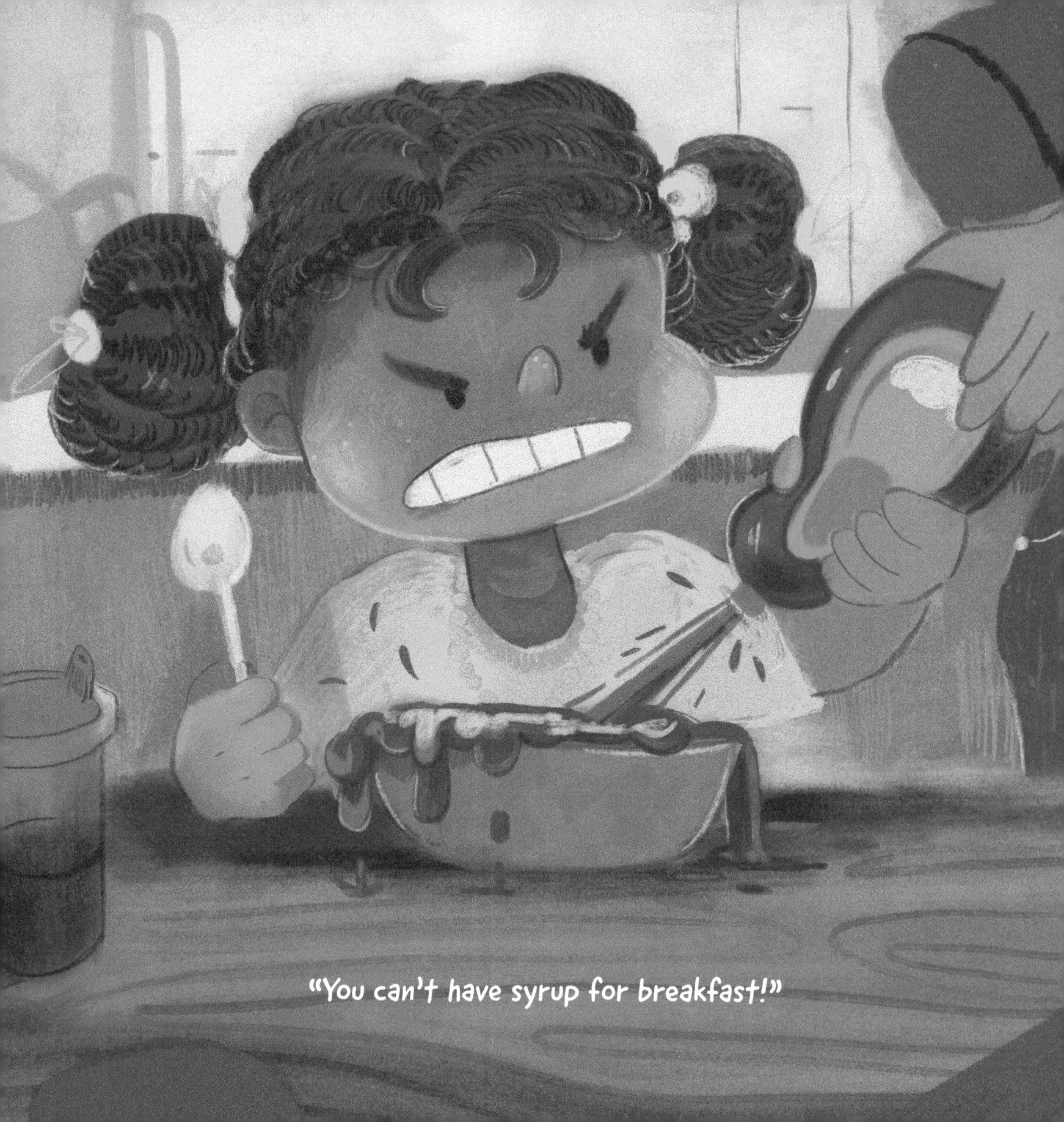

"You can't have syrup for breakfast!"

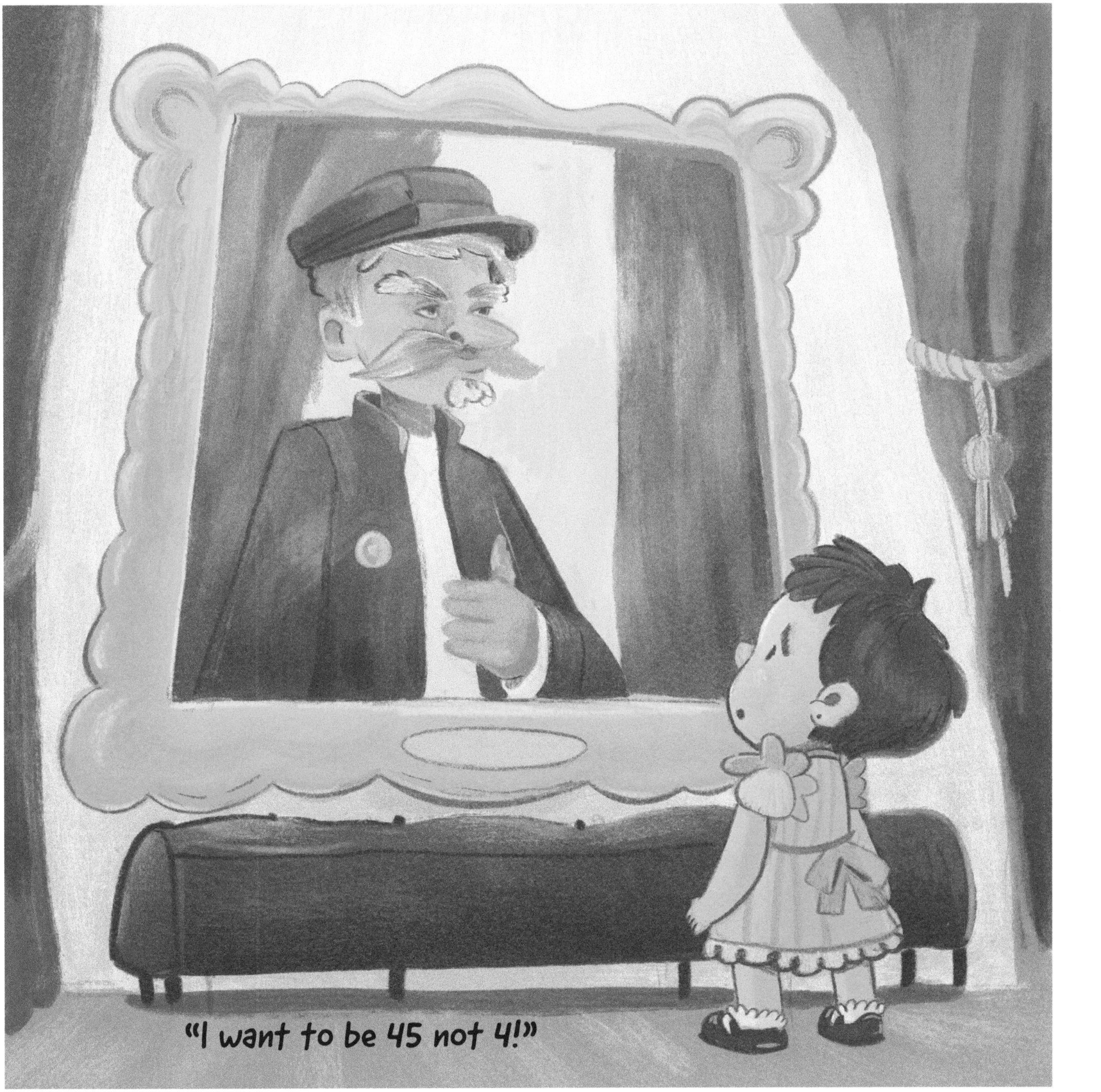
"I want to be 45 not 4!"

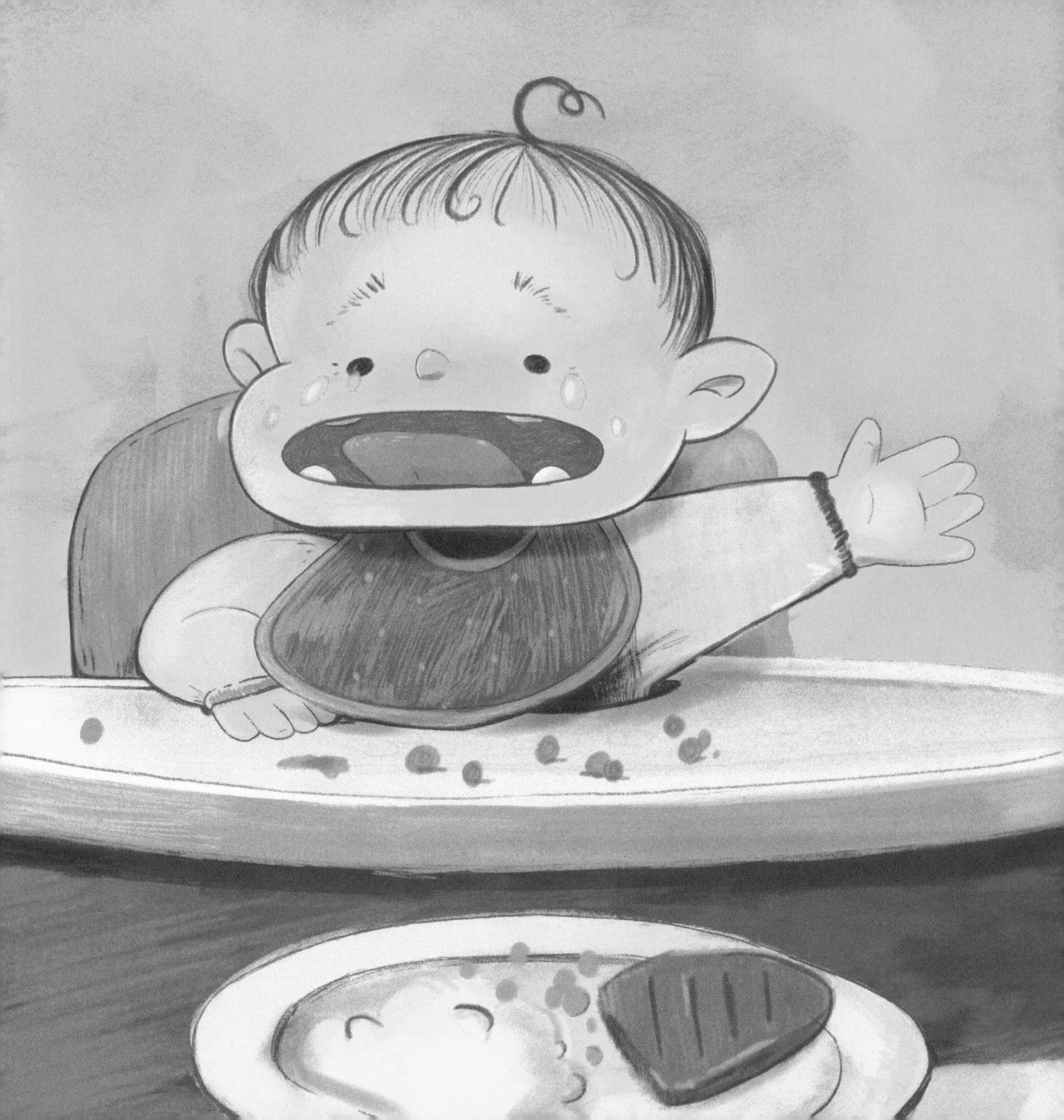

"Don't look at me!!"

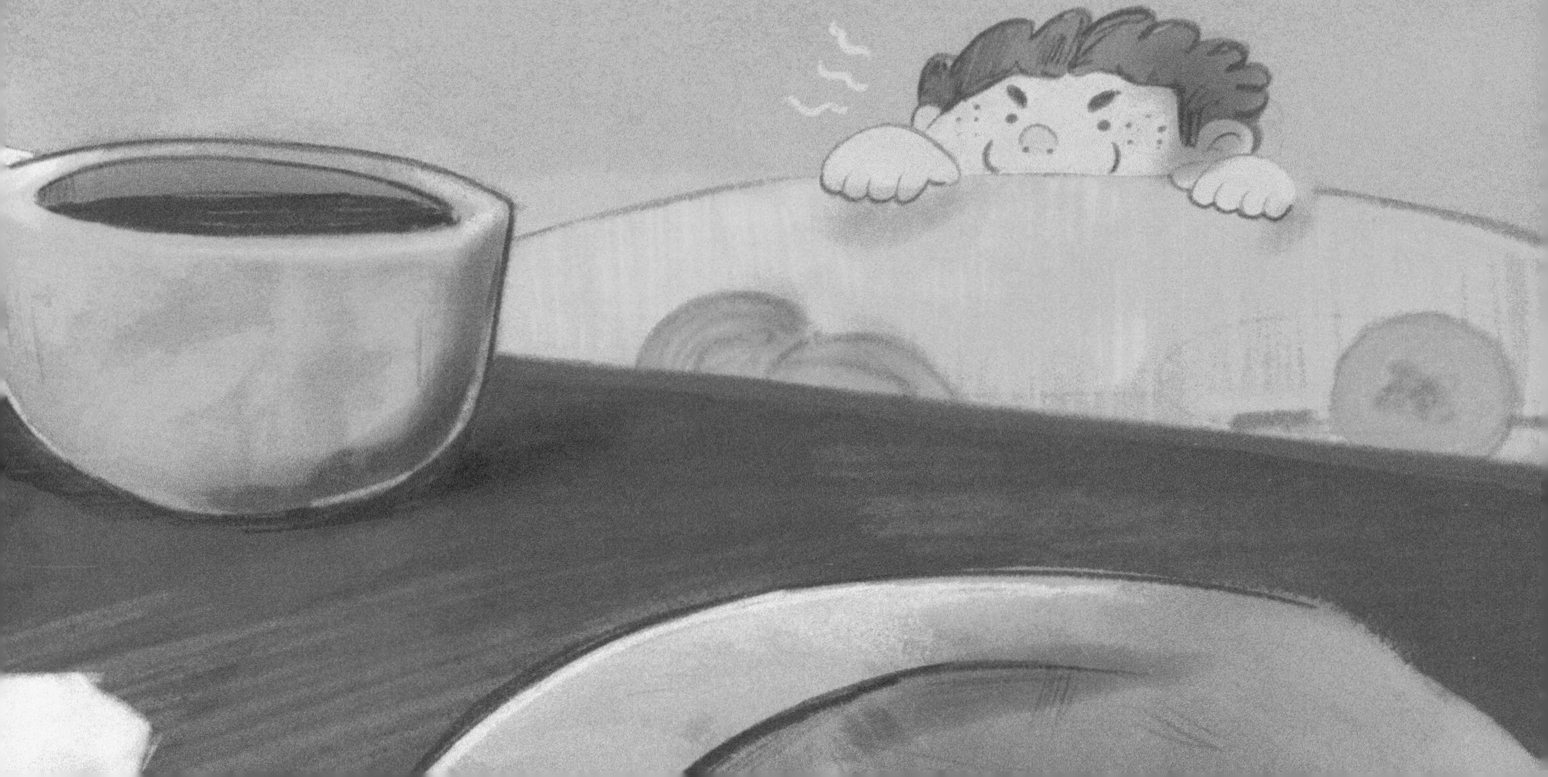

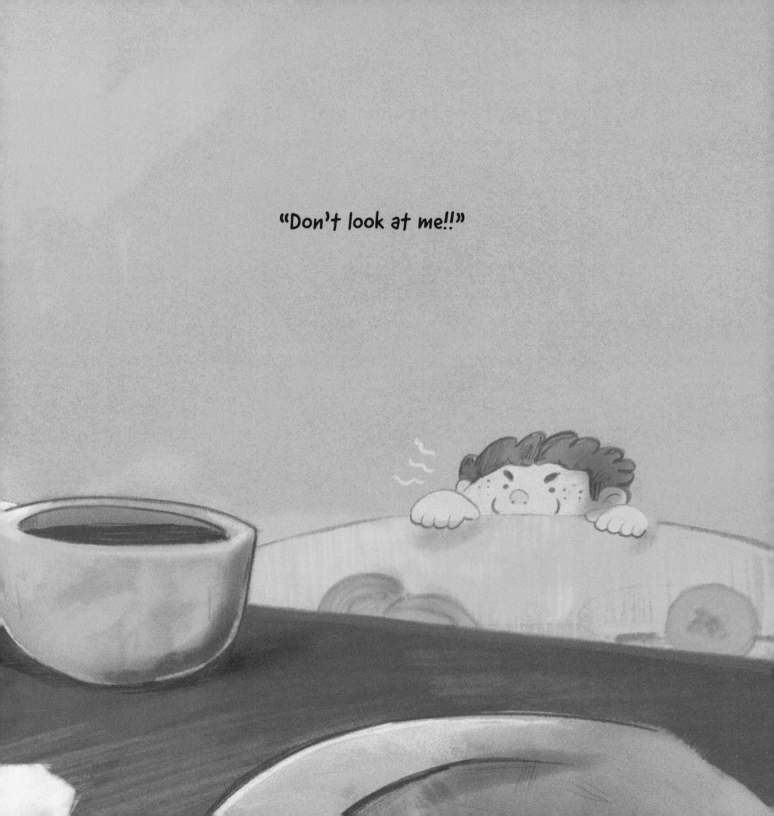

"I can't get the unicorn off my shirt!"

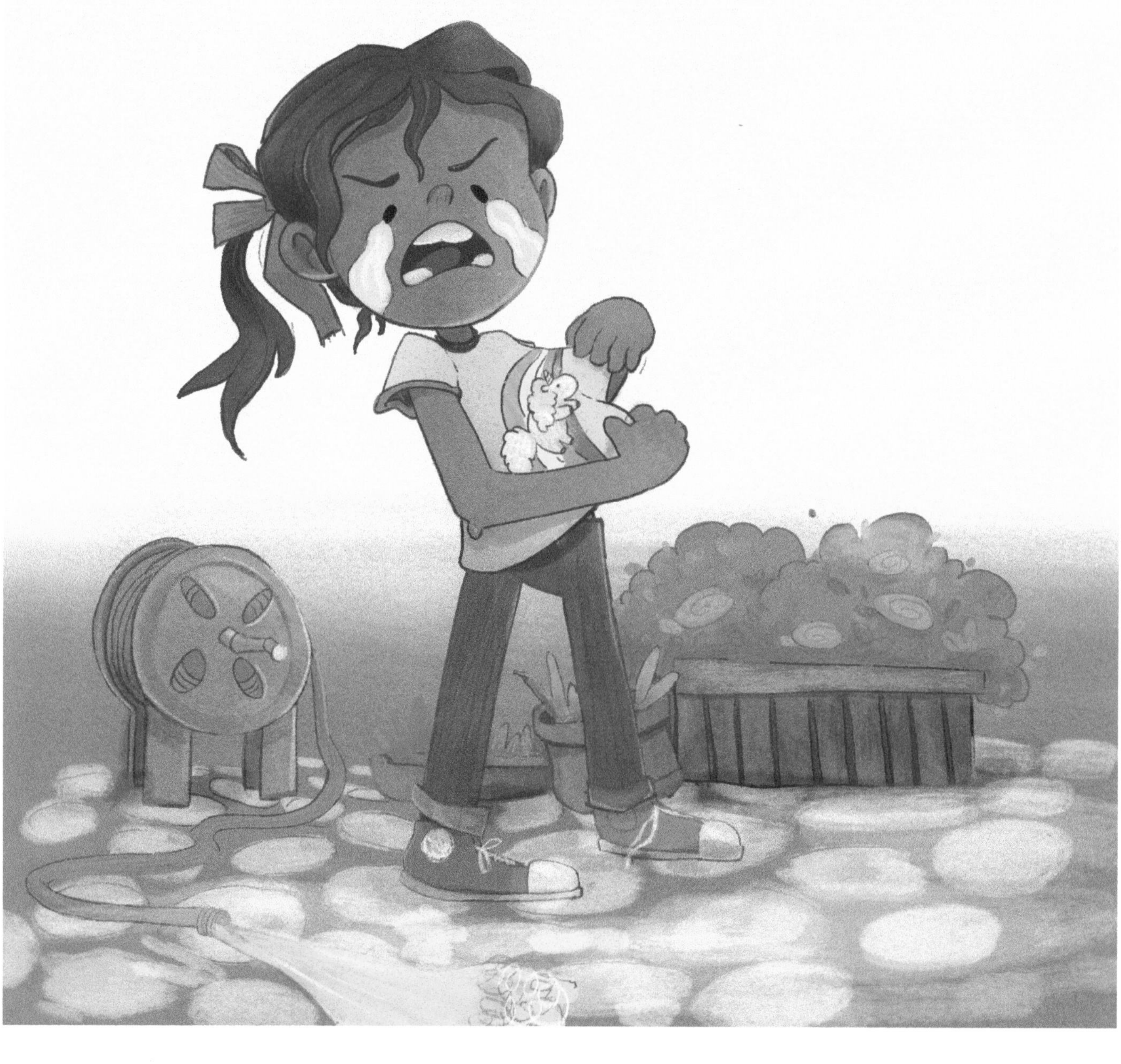

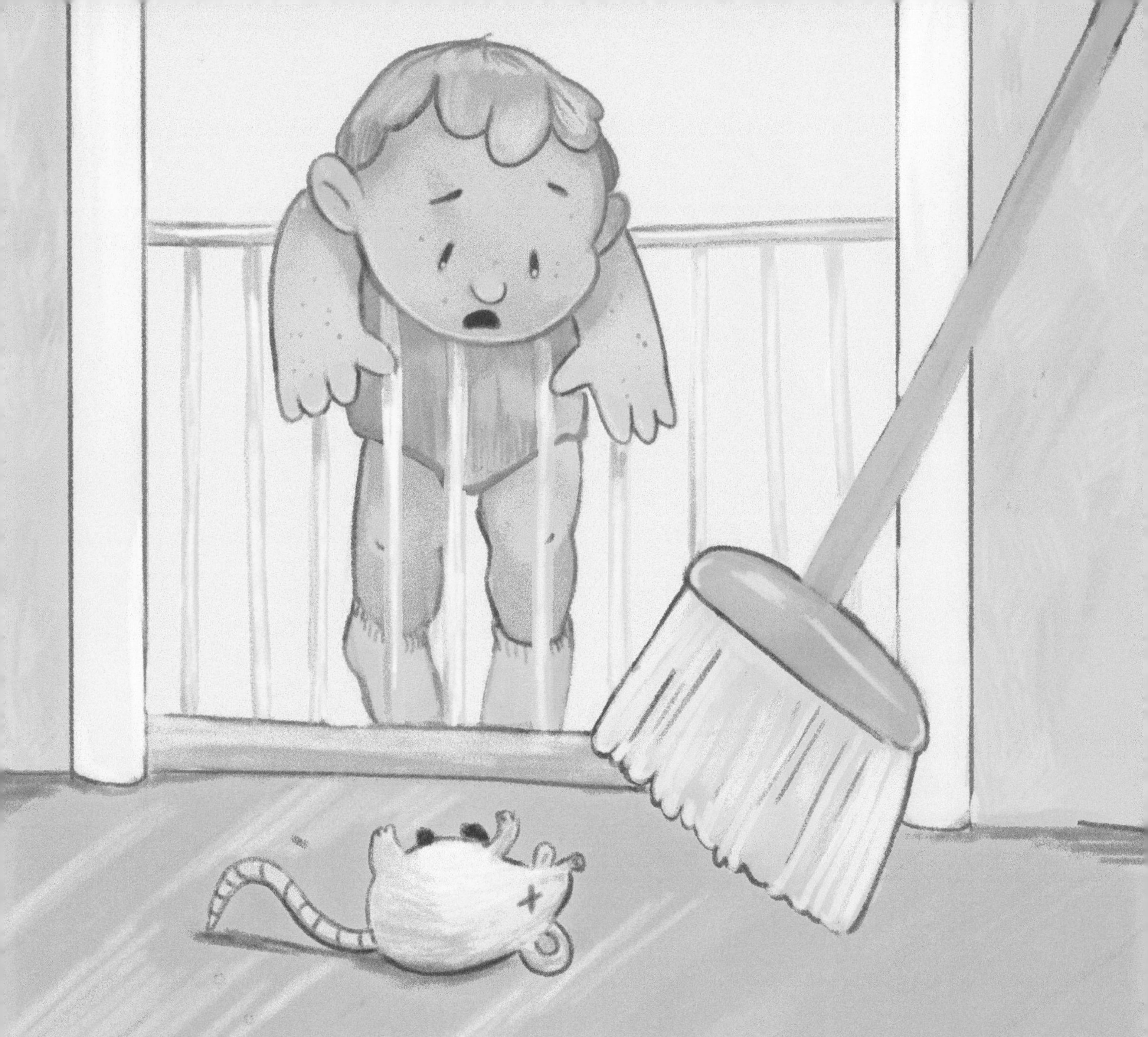

"NO! You can't touch the dead mouse"

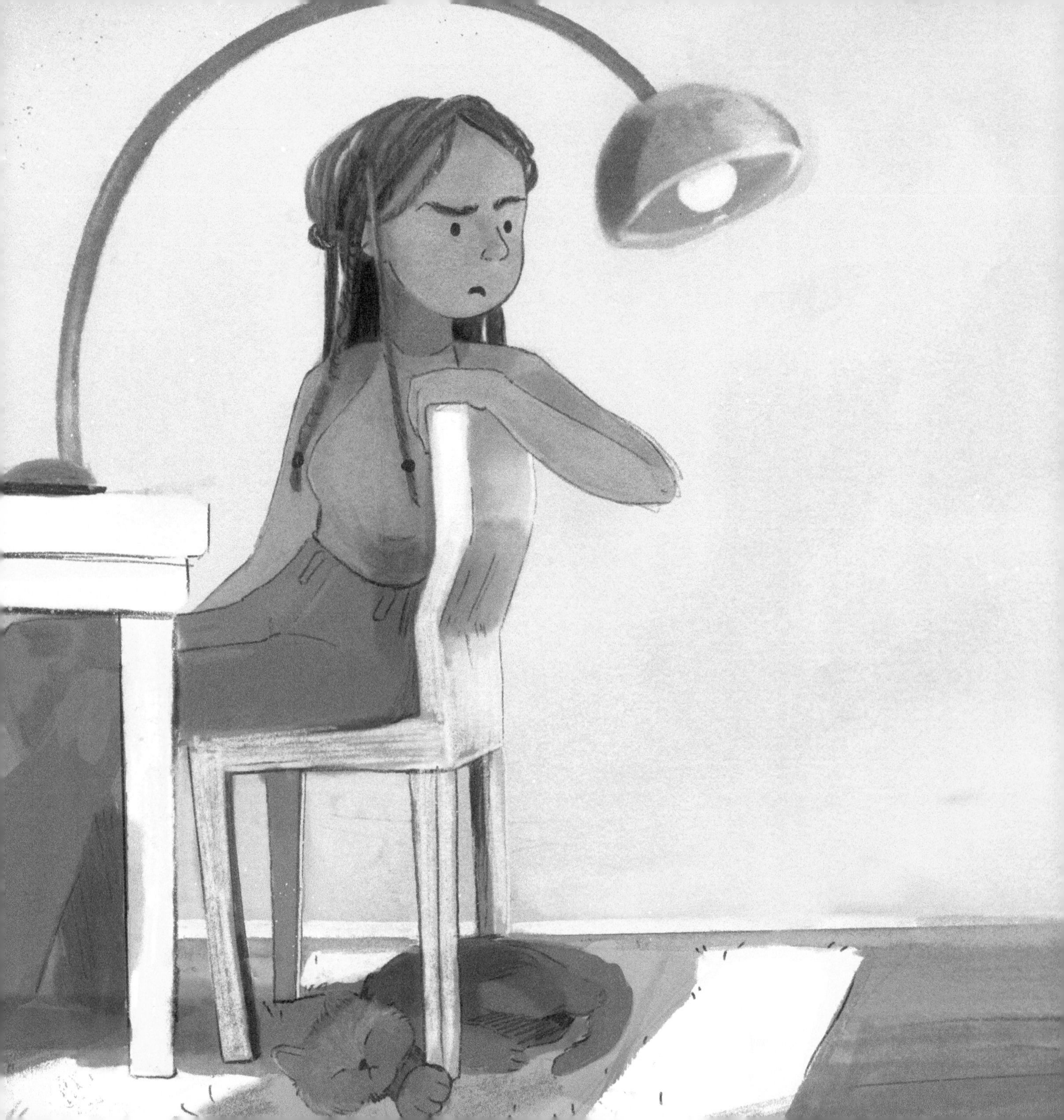

"Why are you crying?"
"You're sitting in the wrong chair."

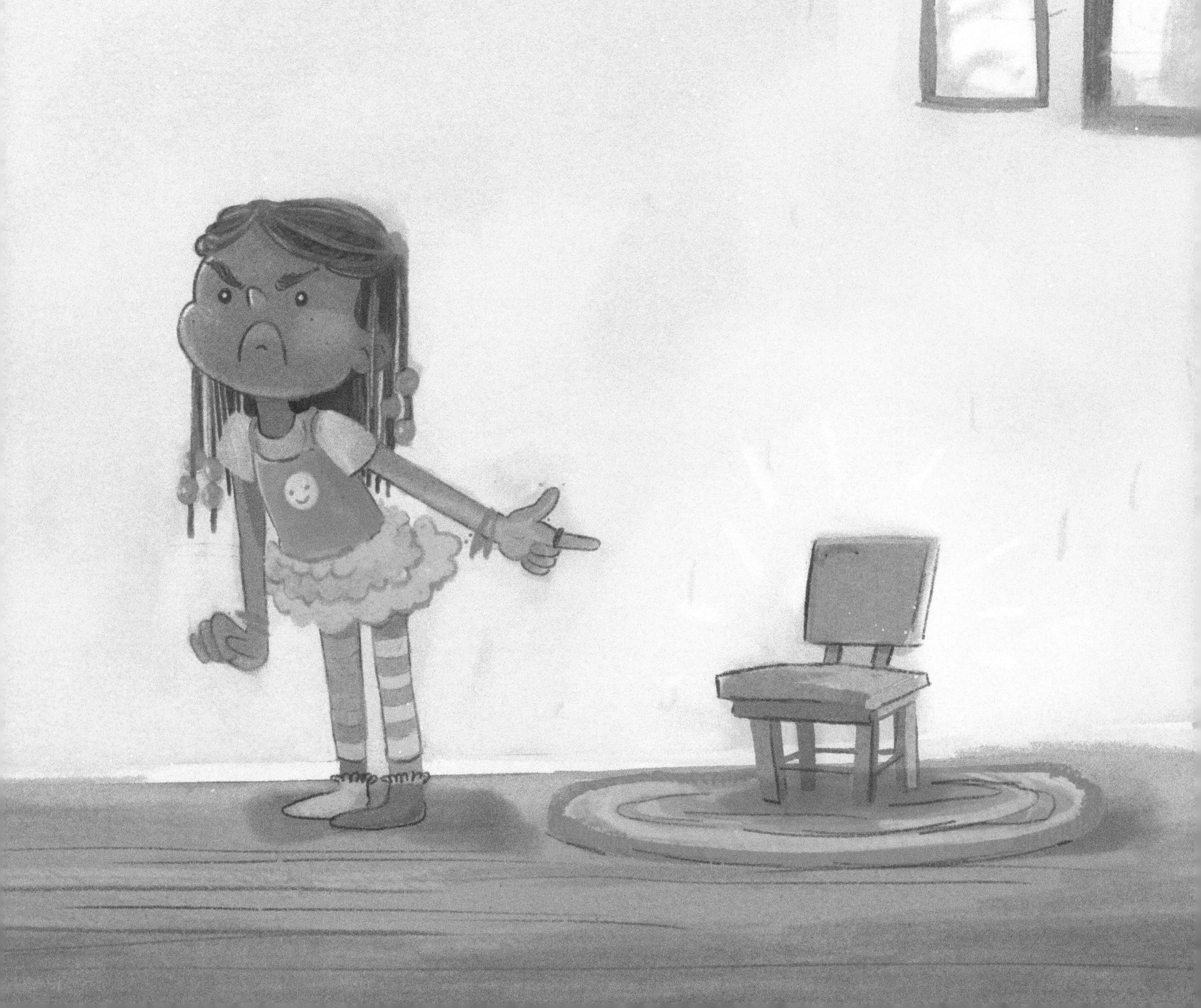

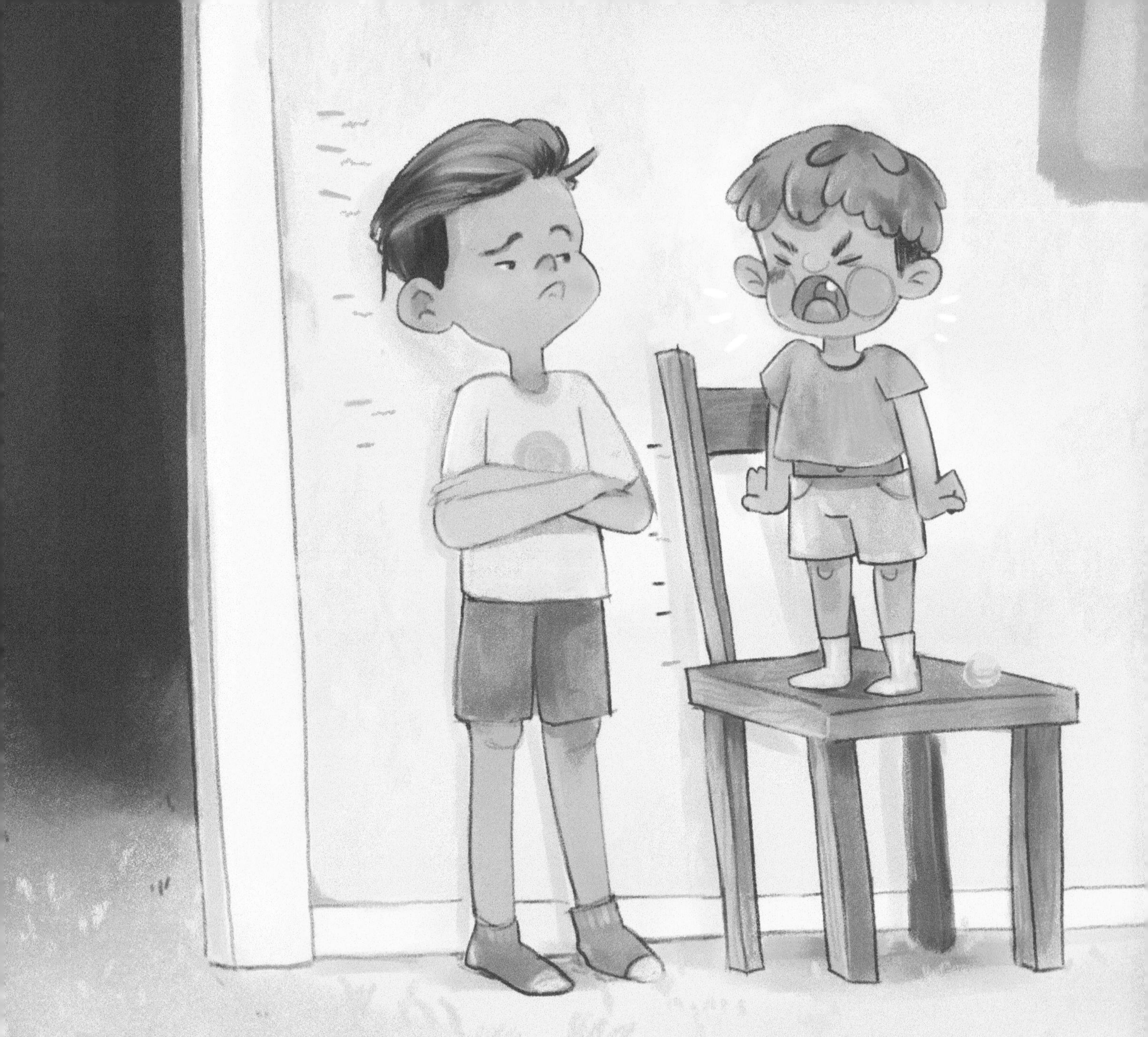

"You can't be older than your brother! He was born first."

"Your blankets not broken, it's just a wrinkle."

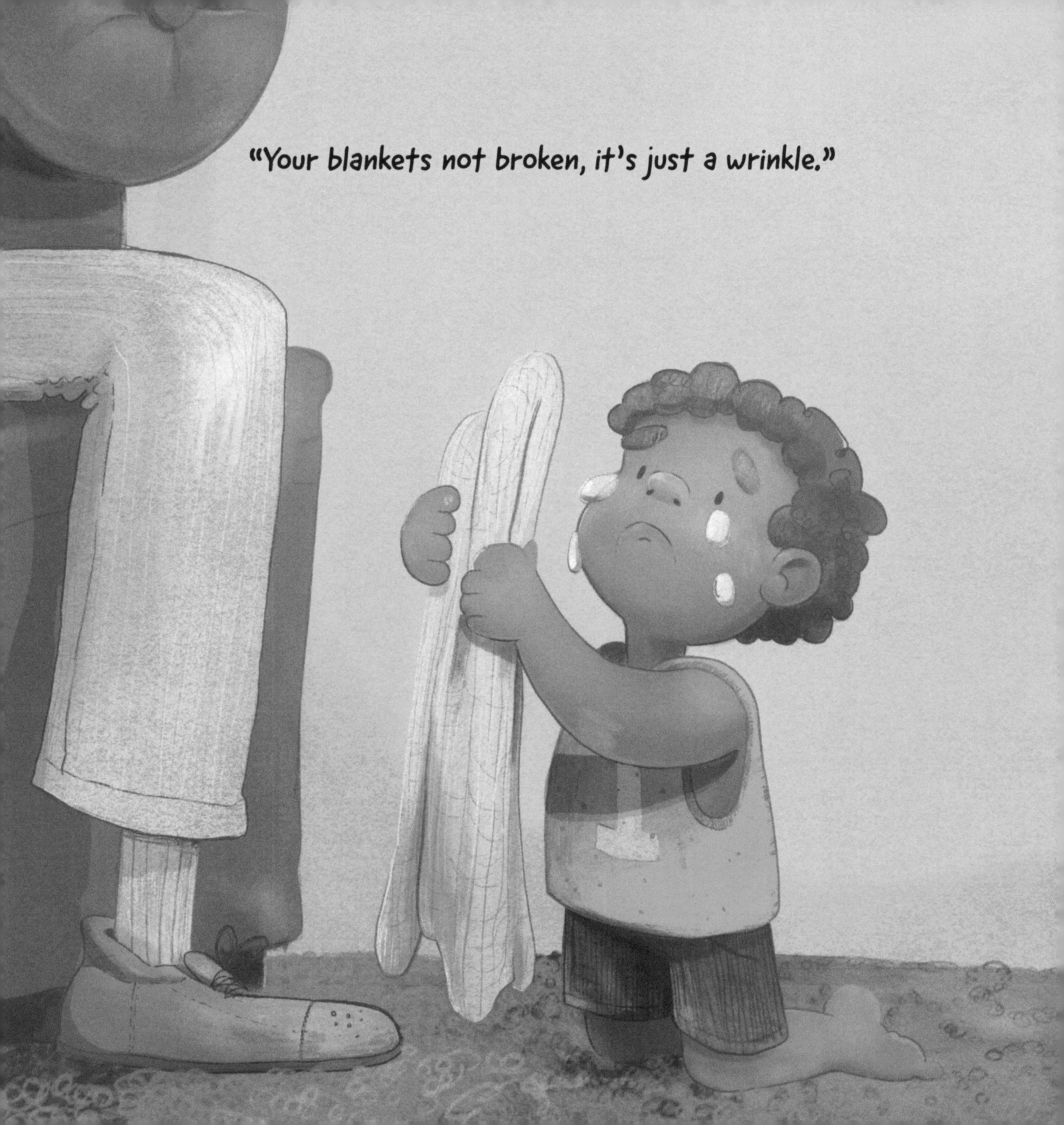

"No! You can't eat crayons!"

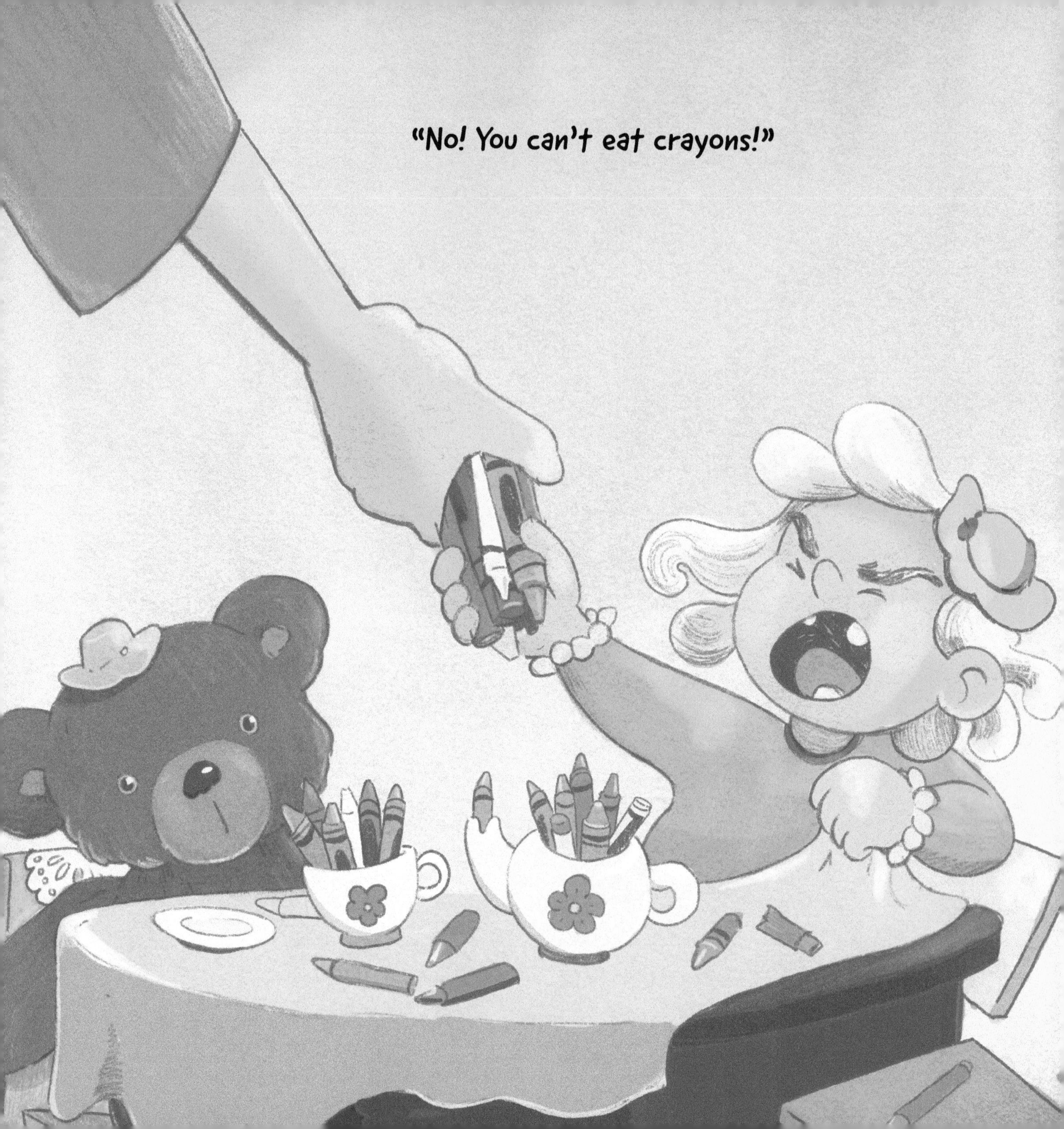

"I'm sorry there's not a squirrel out there right now!"

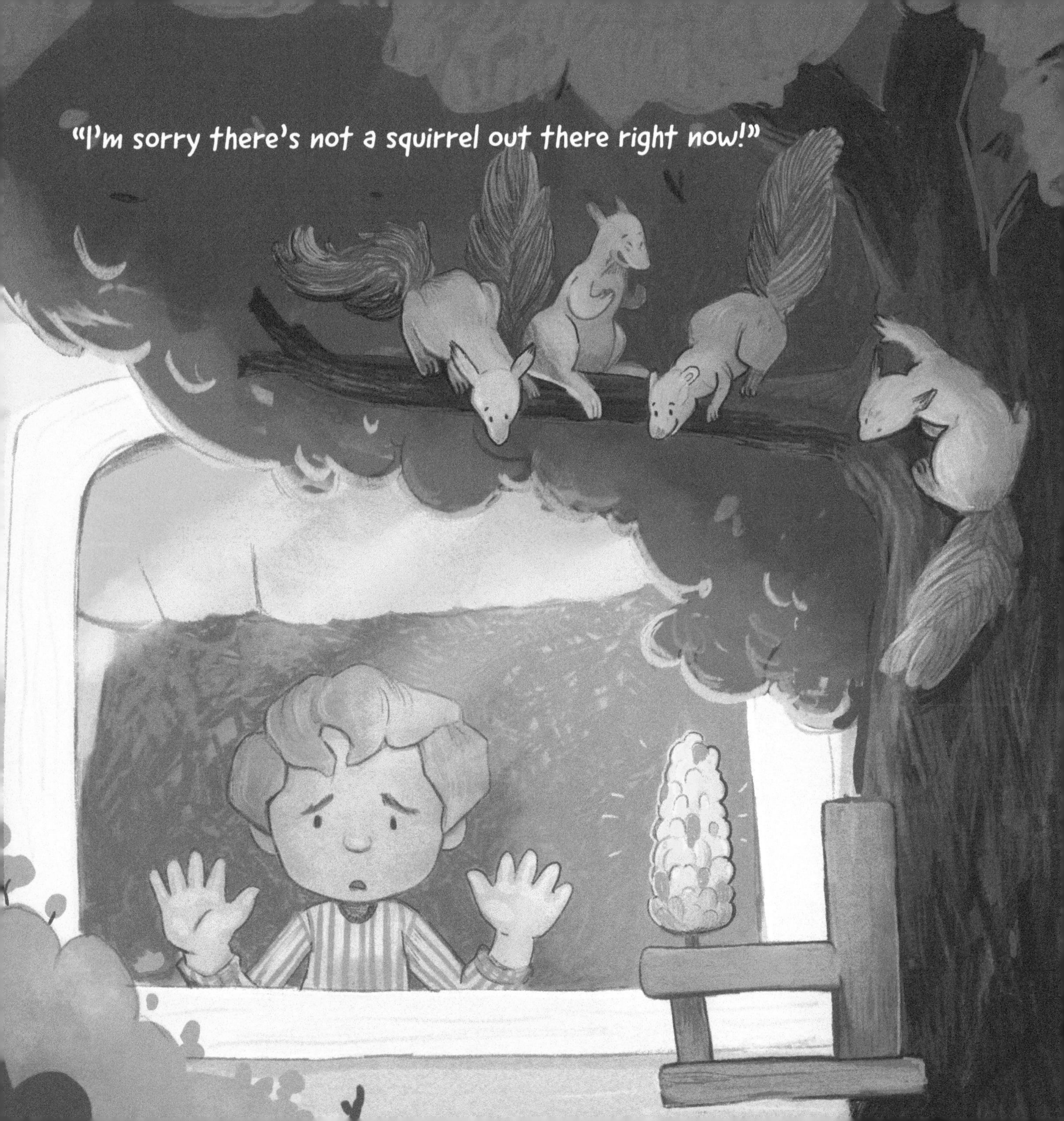

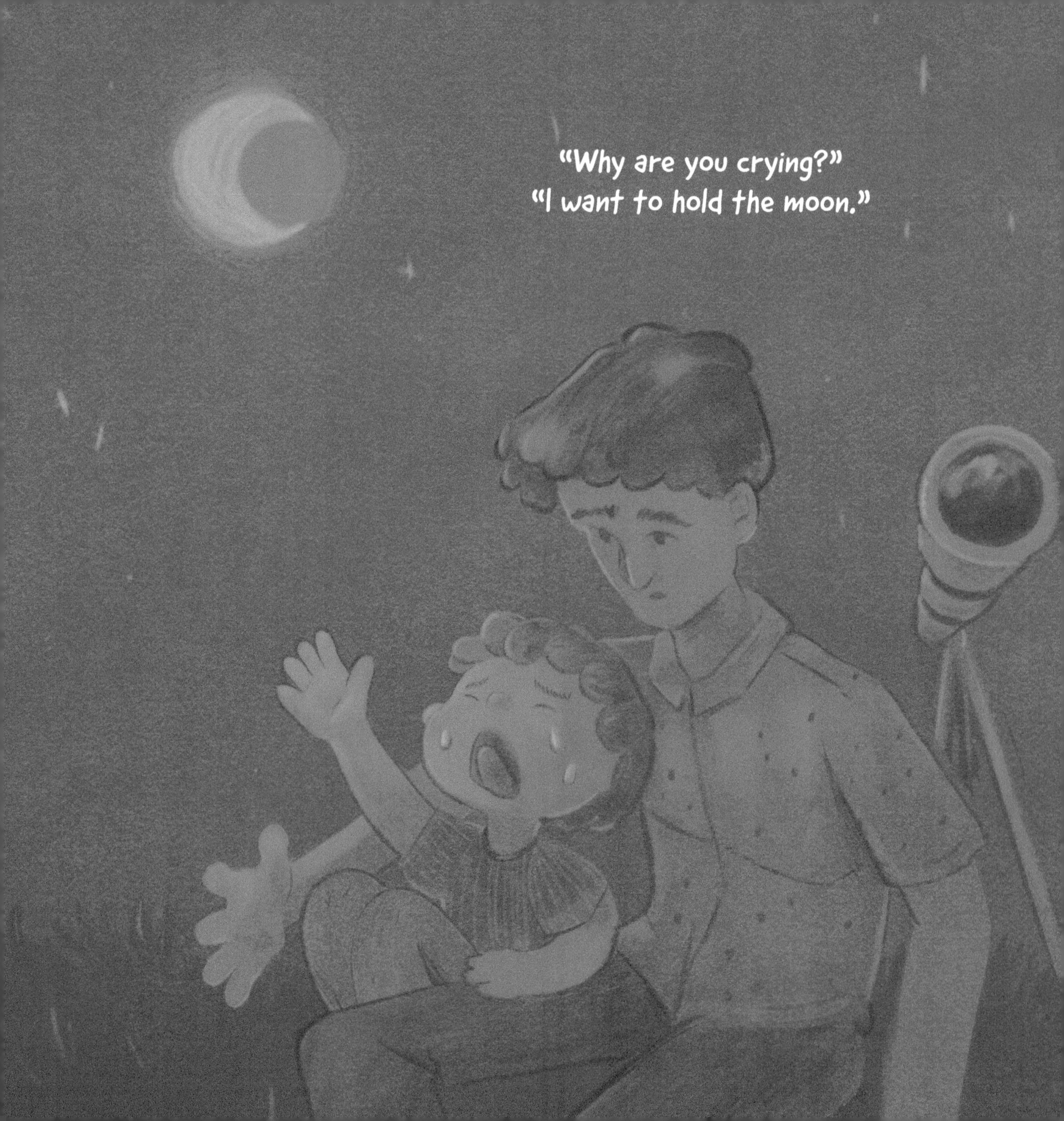
"Why are you crying?"
"I want to hold the moon."

"What's going on back there?"
"He's looking out of my window!"

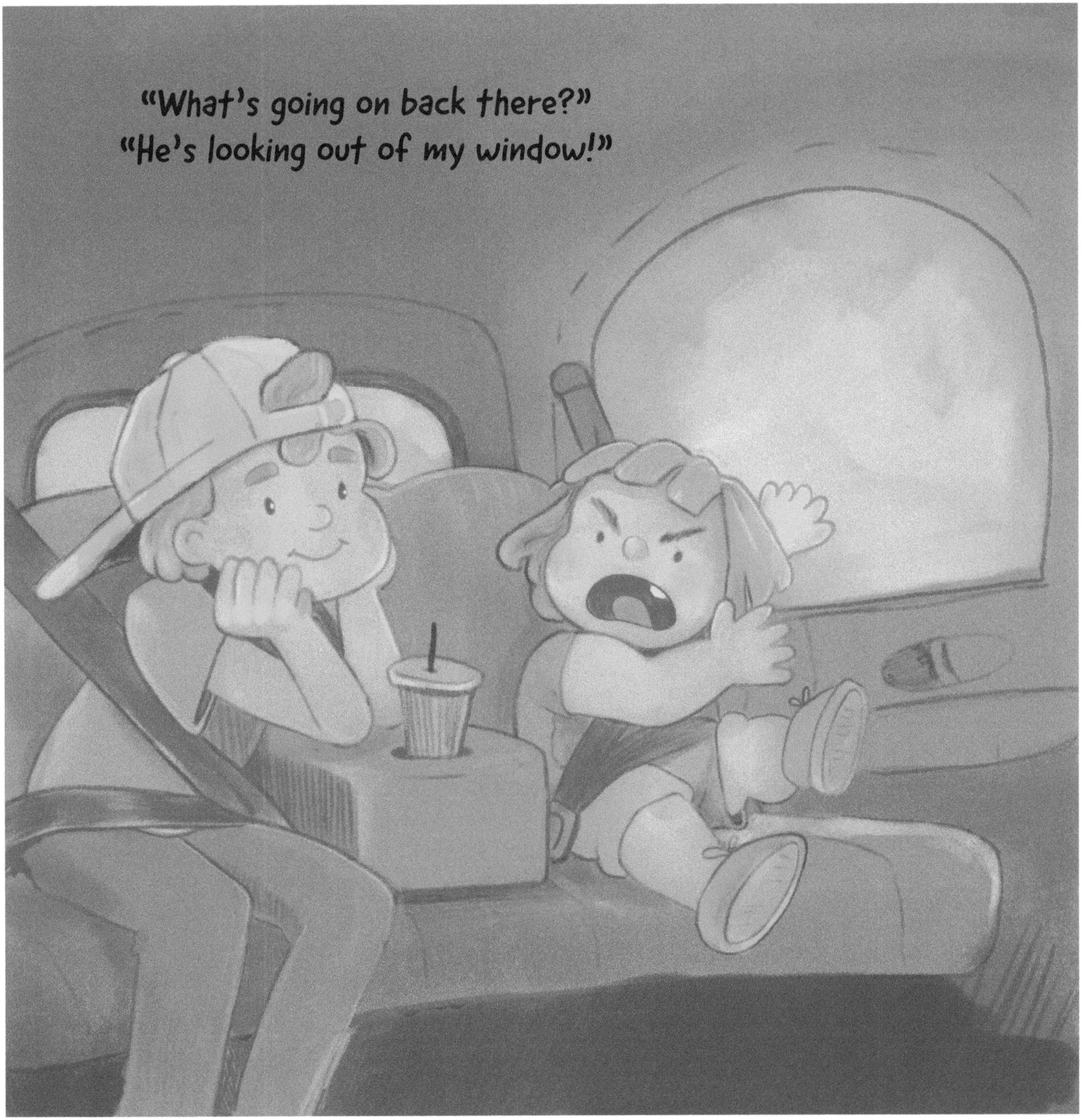

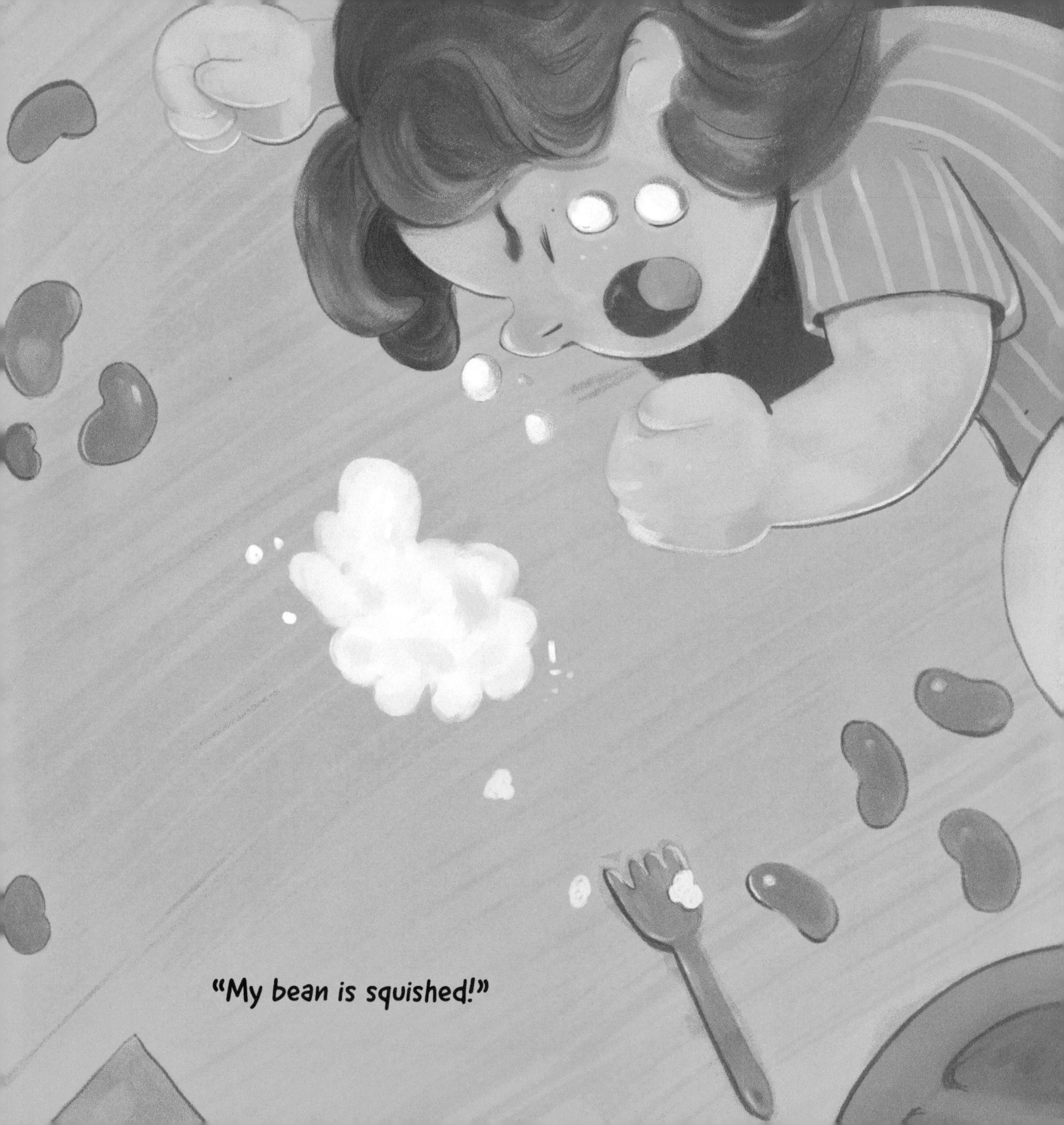

"My bean is squished!"

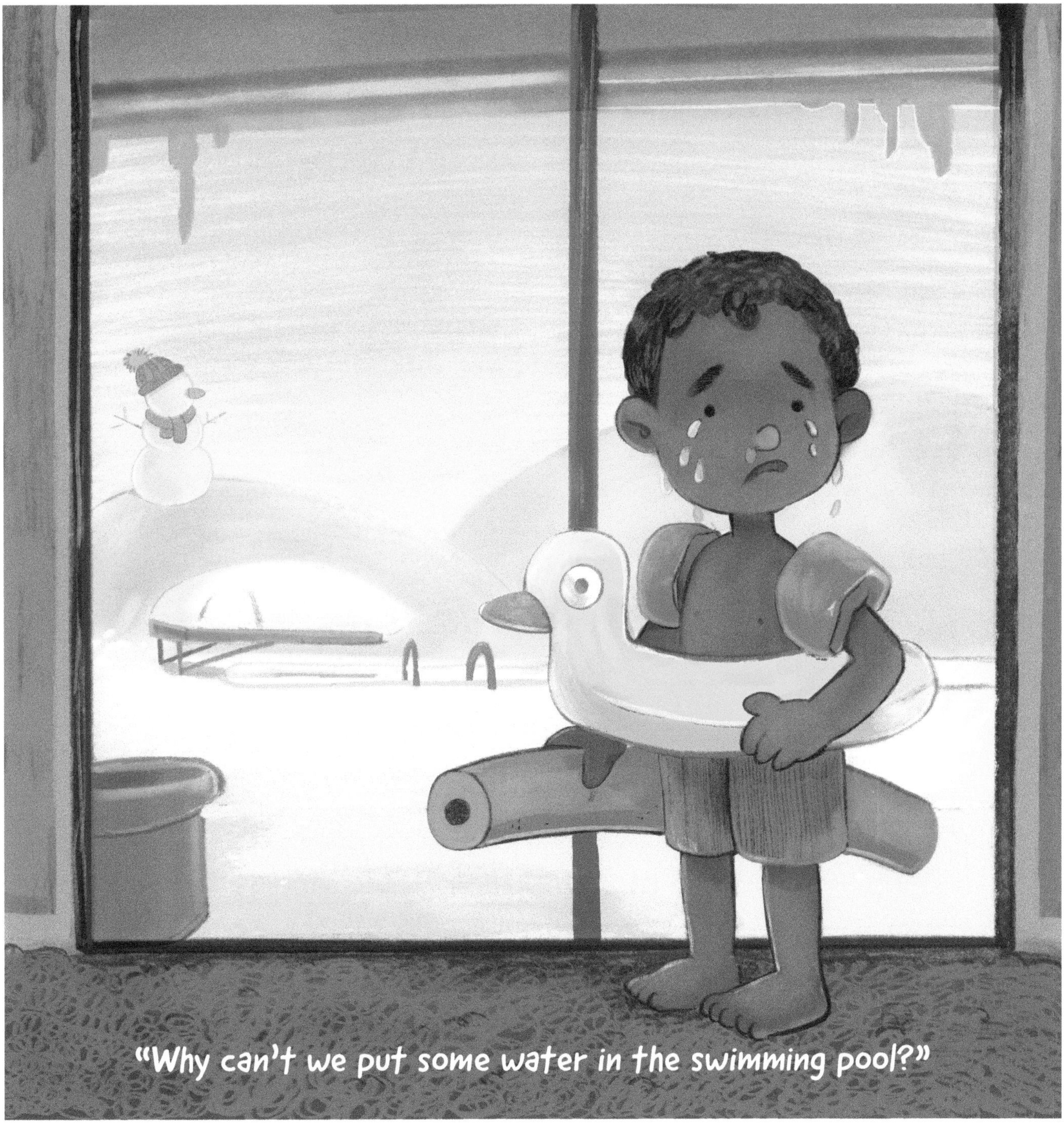

"Why can't we put some water in the swimming pool?"

"No! You can't wash your animals in the toilet!"

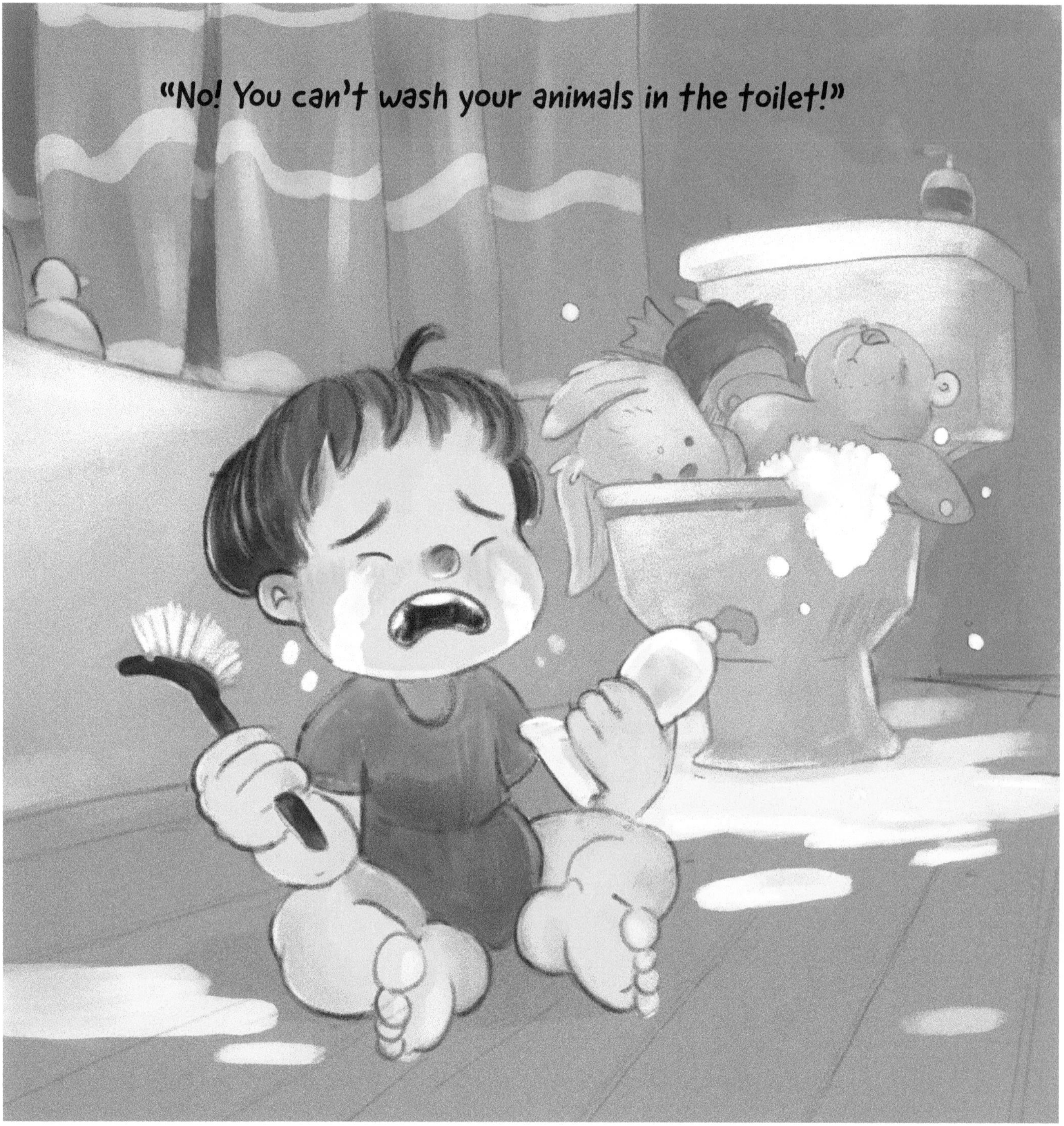

"No, you can't have Cheetos for every meal!"

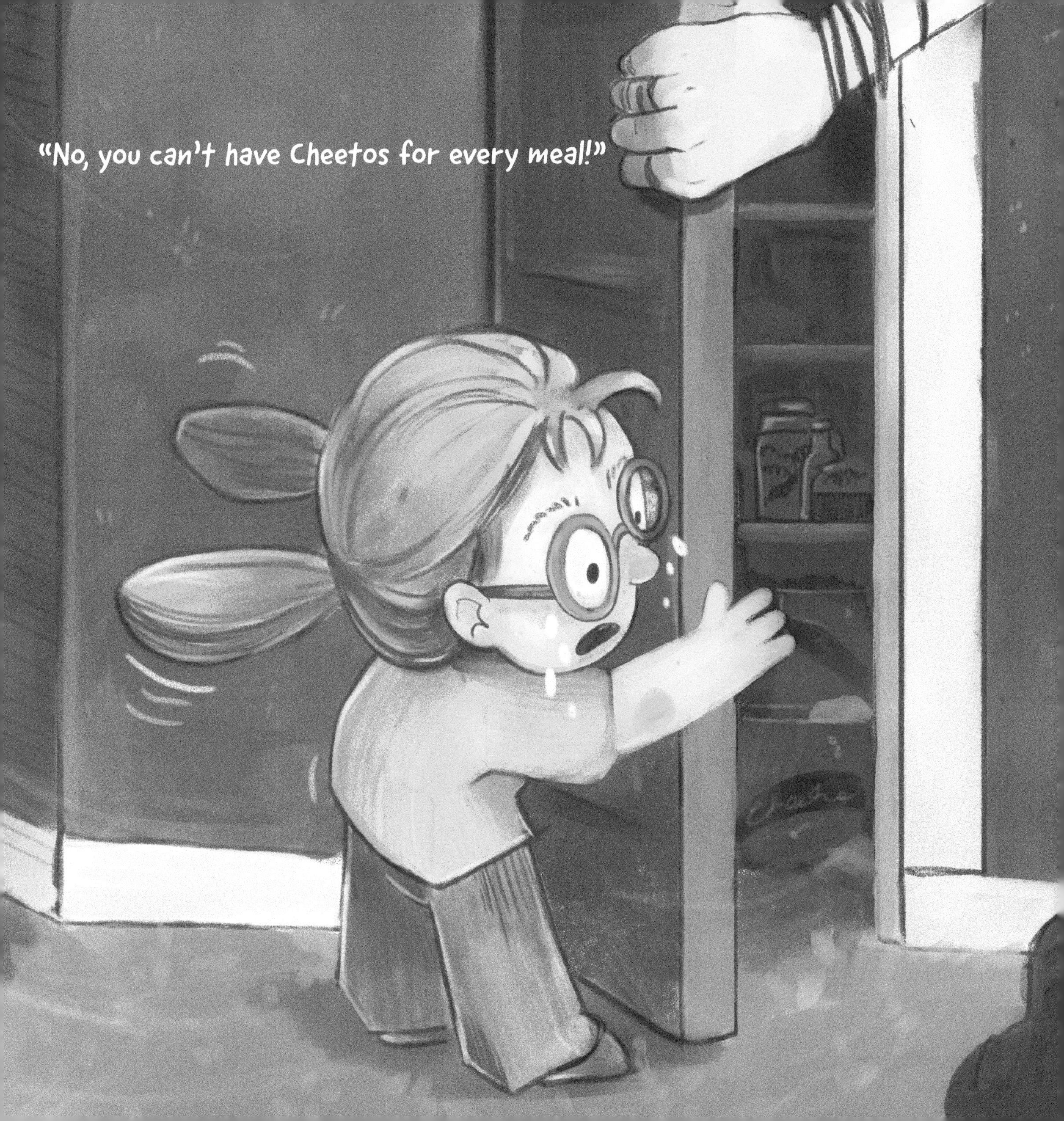

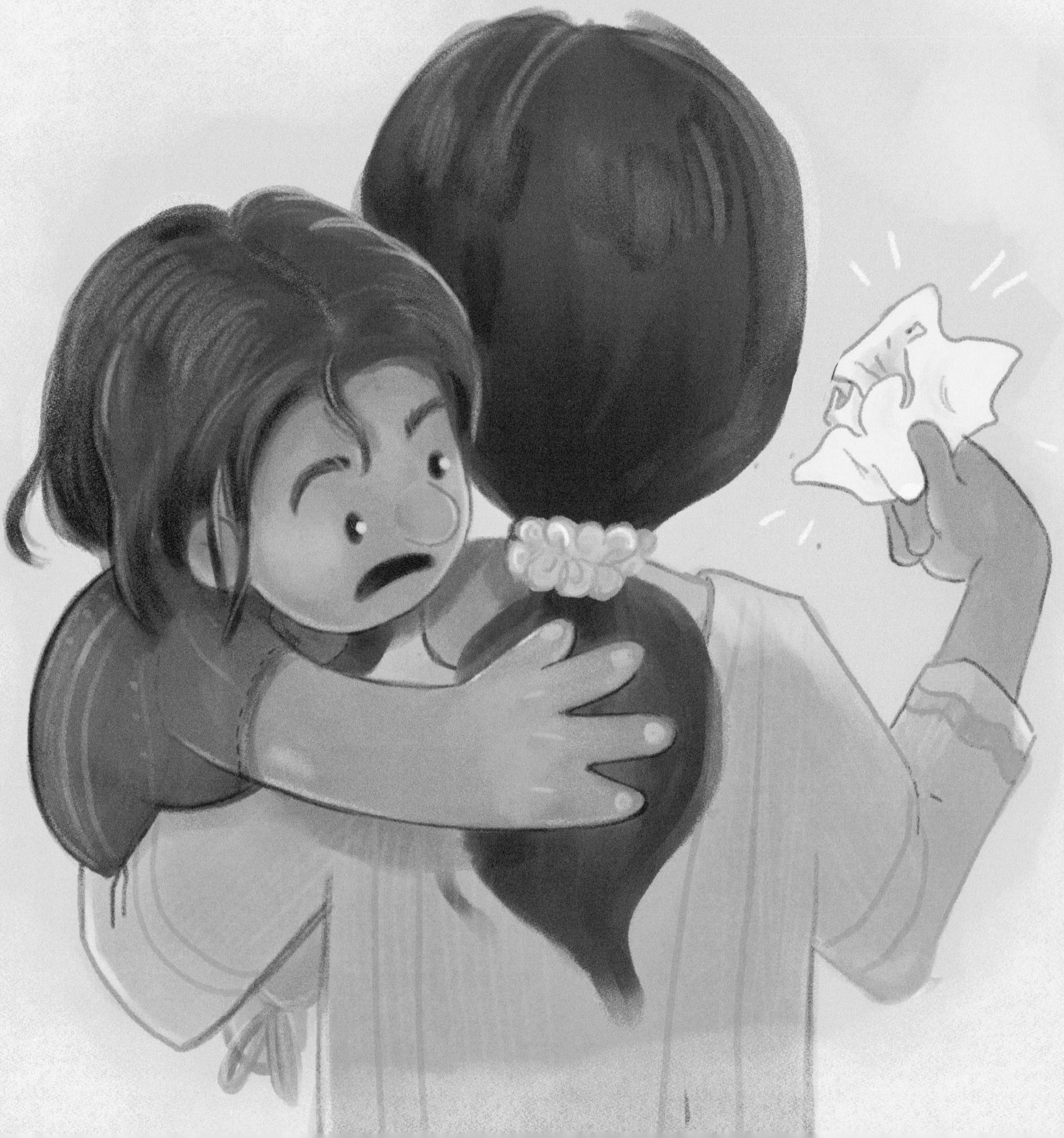

"No, you can't have the booger back on your face!"

See more stories by Debbie L. Hepner and get free coloring
pages at https://debstories.com

Lightning Source UK Ltd.
Milton Keynes UK
UKHW052342090123
415065UK00003B/88

9 781737 506799